UNREAL REAL STORIES

Unreal Real Stories

By Thomas A. Prusak

Writers Club Press
New York Lincoln Shanghai

Unreal Real Stories

Writers Club Press
an imprint of iUniverse, Inc.

For information address:
iUniverse, Inc.
2021 Pine Lake Road, Suite 100
Lincoln, NE 68512
www.iuniverse.com

ISBN: 0-595-25743-7 (pbk)
ISBN: 0-595-65301-4 (cloth)

Printed in the United States of America

Contents

▼

CHAPTER I

MR. LINCOLN, I PRESUME!

On a cold and rainy night when most people are safe and warm in the shelter of their homes relaxing after a good meal in their favorite chair or sofa, I am changing a flat tire with a flash light tucked under my arm on a dark and rainy street. I was on my way back home from my parents, fifty miles away when I had, on such an inappropriate night, this unfortunate situation to deal with.

On completing this task of changing the tire, I slid into the drivers seat feeling like a wet rag with still twenty five miles to drive. I was not in a good mood but finally arrived at my destination, home, an old Victorian house down in the heart of the city. This is where I called home for the last three months, along with three other students who had been there for a year. We all were attending school at the near by college at the time. Climbing the steps to the front door made me feel only a little better but fumbling with my keys and dropping them on the dark porch several times did nothing for my attitude. I had to keep my cool though because everyone else in the house was asleep, as they should be at one A.M...

Once inside, all I could think about was to get off the wet clothes and to take a hot shower, crawl into bed and get a much desired night's sleep. Ignoring the blinking light on the phone answering machine and cat crying for dinner, I headed straight to the bathroom. Just peeling the wet clothes from my rain soaked body was a joy but the shower felt like heaven.

Feeling better as I dried off, I knew I still had to feed the cat before I could caress the warmth and softness of my mattress and pillows. Wrapping myself in a towel and heading for the kitchen I heard the cat still crying for food. Filling her bowls with fresh food and water she finally stopped and began to eat. I turned off the lights in the kitchen and hallway and went to my room. Throwing the towel on the floor and turning back the sheets and covers, I dove into the comfort of my bed, and in a short time I had fallen asleep.

Some time later I had woken up by that irrevocable erge to visit the bathroom. Not really wanting to move, I threw back the covers and stepped out of the warm bed. Grabbing my robe, I headed down the darkened hall toward the bathroom. Being half asleep, I reached out, slightly touching the walls, to find my way. At the same time, I was shuffling my feet and looking down at the floor trying to see so I did not step on the cat if she was laying in her favorite place in the hall.

Half way down the hall and I had not encountered the cat, when all of a sudden my head had bumped up against something. It felt like cloth, wool, I remember thinking. Instantly I figured I had bumped into one of my house mates on their way down the dark hall. Automatically I announced, "Oh, I'm sorry" not hearing a reply, I looked up. What I saw puzzled me for a moment, it was a white shirt and a buttoned suit coat. The white shirt seemed to be hazy and the dark suit coat seemed to have a gray haze or smoke flowing from it almost. Not only that but I was looking directly into the chest of a very tall man. Knowing that not one of my house mates where that tall, I looked up.

What I saw was a man that looked like Abe Lincoln. Not only the traditional white shirt and dark coat, which he worn in those days but he sported a beard and Black Top Hat. I took a half a step back and tried to clear my eyes to get a better look. Yes, that's what I was seeing, an Abe Lincoln figure of a man in full dress. I thought that I must be dreaming but I could feel the coldness of the floor on my bare feet and my hand still touching the wall.

At that instant I had to know if what I was seeing was real and half heartedly swung my hand out in front of me to touch the figure in his chest. To my amazement my hand had passed right through his chest but before I could react or figure out what had happened, he looked down at me and then disappeared into a faint, gray, blue haze.

No, couldn't be. Was that real? If it wasn't anything but my imagination in the shadows of the dark hall, what did I bump my head into because I had certainly felt that. I stepped forward to and continued my journey to the bathroom un-encumbered. Turning on the light in the bathroom I turned around and looked back down the hall but there was nothing there, not even the cat. Not knowing what to make of all this I finished in the bathroom and went back to my room with the aid of the bathroom light that I had left purposely on. Once in bed again I had drifted back off to sleep leaving the mystery to be solved for another day.

The next morning, after waking, I joined my house mates at the kitchen t table for coffee. Then I had remembered what I had experienced the night before in the hall. Not knowing whether to say that I thought I had seen a ghost of Abe Lincoln or not, I came out and said that I had a strange dream last night. I dreamed that I had ran into Abe Lincoln in the upstairs hall. When all of a sudden John blurts out, "You saw Abe last night?" I was taken totally by surprise with his question. He continued, "You're the third person this year." "What?", I asked, in amazement. "What do you mean the third person this year?" John says, "Yea, you're the third person this year to see Abe in that hall this year. I've been here for two years and have never seen him, you lucky dog." John goes on to say that when he rented the house two years ago, for students, from an old man, that he old man had asked to him to say hi to Abe. John says he did not understand the old man at the time but soon did, when the first student saw Abe three months later in that hall one night. John also said that there were only two sightings last year but that now there was three this year with my sighting.

I couldn't believe it. I had seen a ghost and not just an ordinary ghost but a ghost that looked like Abe Lincoln. It seems that the old man, upon John's questioning he, said that Abe had been seen numerous times over the thirty years he owned the house. Not wanting to scare John, as a renter, away, he held back on mentioning the sightings. The man had told him that Abe has never hurt or caused anyone any harm over the years and that he could not find out what he was doing in this house. This did not scare John away so he continued to rent the home. John admits that he doesn't tell new people about Abe and just waits to see their reaction too either seeing or hearing about him.

I had moved out of the house to go to college in another state after that year. I remember feeling kind of privileged to have seen Abe while I was there. I remember even looking for him some nights in that hall but to no avail. Abe had made his last appearance to anyone for that year. As I fell out of touch with John over the following year, I often wondered how many more unsuspecting students had been surprised by a hazy figure of a man, in that dark hall, a hazy figure of a man that looked remarkably like Abe Lincoln.

The End

▼

CHAPTER 2

DOG GONE

Downtown Detroit is where I was living, the old part of the city, where strange things can happen. I rented a room in an old Victorian home. It was quaint and cozy with wooden floors, large staircase and wooden banisters. I shared this house with four other people. We all had our own rooms. One day a friend, Ed, came over to say hi and spend the day hanging out with me. I was feeling a little under the weather so I had stayed home from school. No one else was there, either being at their jobs, at college classes or doing their errands.

Ed and I had been sitting on the front porch when Tank, a renter at the house, pulls up the driveway with a dog in his car. It was a small German Shepherd. The dog bound out of the car as Tank opened the door. The dog ran directly up to Ed and me on the porch like we were all old friends. Having never seen this dog before I figured he was just an overly friendly dog. Tank said he was watching the dog for his girl friend of his while she was at work. The dog was very friendly so we continued to welcome him. His name was Scooter

We all hung out for while on the porch when Tank says he had to run some errands and could we watch the dog for a few hours. We said, sure why not. We had planned to stay at the house anyway and the dog was having a good time with us. After Tank left we took the dog for a walk and a run in the park. On the way back we even bought him a hamburger when we stopped for a bite to eat. When we got back to the house we went inside and watched some television, the dog lay on the floor beside us looking very content.

It was getting dark when Tank got home. SLAM! Goes the car door. Boom, boom, boom, his foot steps sounded as they he made his way up the old Victorian wooden porch steps. SLAM, goes the front door to the house. "WHERE'S MY DOG?", he lets out in a loud voice. We could tell he was not in a good mood, to say the least. Tank comes stomping through the house into the living room where we sat with the dog. In his deep gruffly voice, he commands the dog, "COME HERE." The dog first cowered under the coffee table but as Tank reached for him, he took off, down the wood-floored hall on the first floor and up the stairs to the second floor. As Tank takes off after the dog he yells, "Damn it, I said COME HERE!" No good, the dog doesn't even slow down.

Needless to say Tank chased after the dog. We could hear the chase continue through the second floor hallway. The clicking of the dogs toenails and stomping of Tank's big boots could not be missed. He chased the dog all through the house for about 20 minutes. The dog and Tank were diving under tables, knocking over chairs, messing up the throw rugs scattered in the living room where the chase had started. What a scene this had become. He did not hurt the dog through all this, never even got close enough to touch him. So Ed and I just sat back and watched the whole scene, all the time rooting for the dog. Finally, Tank catches the dog, slings him under his arm and starts heading for his room on the third floor. SLAM goes the door that lead to the third floor room from the second floor hallway. CLUMP, CLUMP, CLUMP, up the small stairway we hear them go. It was a wood stairway and floor also, so we could hear every step. Tank puts the dog down and tells him to go lay down. We hear the dog walking, because his claws where 'clicking' on the wood floor over to where he was going to lie down. Plop, we hear the weight of the dogs body hit the floor.

Now that all the excitement was over Ed and me, after picking up the knocked over chairs, decided to listen to some music in my room. My room was on the second floor, an opposite end of the house, down the hall from Tank's stairway to the third floor. We sat down on the floor on either side of the door. From our vantage points we could each only see a few feet into the hall. Then to our surprise, before the music had started, we heard the dog coming down the hall toward my room., Click, Click, Click, we could hear his nails on the wooden floor. Ed and I both looked at each other, smiling, and thought Al right, he broke out! Good for him, I thought. We were excited to see that he had escaped from his tyrant kidnapper. I had noticed how we did not hear him coming down the stairs to the second floor but I did not pay it too much attention at that time

Here he comes, Click, Click, Click. As the sounds came closer, we focused on the doorway. Click, Click, Click, they got louder and louder as he got closer to my doorway. As the sounds entered the carpet of the room the Clicking was muffled, as it should be from the cushioning of the carpeting. He dropped himself onto the floor between us to lie down and we heard the weight of his body again hit the floor along with his sigh of relief. Well, you would think that is the end of this story but it's not. There was only one thing wrong with this picture. There WAS NO DOG THERE TO BE SEEN! Nothing! We were looking at the carpet only, that's all that was there. I blinked but saw nothing. Ed and I looked each other in disbelief. We did not know what to believe, had we gone blind or where we dreaming. We stayed silent in awe. We were thinking the same thing and did not have to say a word to know it. The dog's spirit must have made it back to us. His draw to us was so strong that he wanted to be with us again. There was nothing else to believe because there was nothing to see there before us. As I sat there, I thought, well, maybe we were old friends after all.

The End

CHAPTER 3

▼

BOB'S BLESSING

"O.K., now go lay down," Bob said to Streak, the white German Shepherd. The dog hung his head and walked across the room to his bed to lie down. Bob had just come back from a training lesson with the Shepherd. He was in the process of finishing attack training with Streak. Streak graduated in two weeks. Streak was close to the top of his class. Bob had owned the dog for three years and Streak was the family pet. Now he could know for sure his family would have good protection when he was on the road as an Interstate truck driver.

Ashley, Bob's daughter, was just getting in from school. She was 12 years old. Ashley had been learning to cook family meals from Jan, her mother, and today was her day to show off what she had learned. She was making a pot roast with all the trimmings. She was so excited. Ashley changed from her school clothes and headed for the kitchen to start preparing the meal. Pots and pans were clanking as she dug them out of the cabinets. Silverware and dinner plates could be heard being placed down on the counter also. This not only had gotten Bob's attention but also Streaks.

Bob asked Ashley to take it easy explaining that there was plenty of time for her to finish making the meal before mom came home from work. Streak, without Bob noticing, got up and walked into the kitchen. He knew that food was about to be pulled out and he couldn't resist the temptation to get a better whiff of it. After all he had a good excuse to be in the kitchen, that's where his food bowl was. He knew better than to beg for food so he wisely walked over to his food and water bowls first. Ashley was continuing to prepare the food.

She had all her utensils, pots, pans, dishes, vegetables and meat on the counter tops. She was feeling so proud to be able to cook for Mom and Dad, just like a big girl. Streak had snuck over and sat down with his nose inches away from the counter top. The raw Pot Roast was to his left on the counter. Ashley was buzzing around the kitchen in a world of her own. She walked over to the counter on the right of Streak and began working. The meat was next. It had to be seasoned. Ashley put the roasting pan in place and reached in front of Streak for the pot roast. Streak had been smelling that roast for too long, temptation over came him and he lunged at Ashley's arm. Grabbing her forearm and like he was taught in school, he held on and shook it violently. Ashley was screaming and Streak was growling.

Bob, hearing the commotion jumped out of his chair, newspaper flying and ran toward the kitchen. Yelling the Off Command as he entered through the doorway to the kitchen, he couldn't believe the horror before his eyes. Streak lets go as Bob grabs him by the neck, picks him up and hurls him across the kitchen away from Ashley. Ashley, now laying on the floor, is bleeding from her arm profusely. Bob grabs a kitchen towel and makes a tourniquet on Ashley's arm as quick as possible to slow the bleeding. He picked her up and runs to the front door to get to the car and the hospital. He never looked back to see if the dog was even alive after his flight across the kitchen and into a wall, Bob didn't care about Streak at this point.

Bob was really shook up, as one would be after such an incident, as he drove as fast as he could, to the nearby hospital. The Emergency personnel took her to the front of the line and doctors and nurses began to work on her immediately. Bob was escorted to the waiting room by a consoling nurse. In the waiting room Bob began weeping and praying. "How and why did this happen? Oh my God, oh my God." A half an hour had passed when the doctor came in to give Bob the report on Ashley. "Sit down Bob." The doctor commanded, "your daughter is going to be all right." "Let me assure you that we are doing everything possible for your daughter." Then he adds, "her arm is pretty badly mangled and may have to be amputated." At hearing this Bob burst out. "What, Oh my God no!, No!, No!, Oh my God no." "There may still be a chance for her to keep it, we'll just have to wait until morning to see how it's doing," the doctor told Bob in an attempt to calm him down. It didn't work. Bob was a hysterical wreck.

Jan, Bob's wife, after seeing the blood at home, raced to the hospital. Upon arriving and questioning the nurse at the counter, she was lead to the waiting room and joined with Bob. Jan had already been informed of Ashley's condition and prognoses. They stayed in the hospital until almost midnight. Ashley was sleeping from the excitement and the medication for hours now. Bob and Jan decided to go home for the night and check with the doctors in the morning. There wasn't anything they could do for Ashley right now. When they got home Bob found 'Streak' conscious, probably bruised but good enough to walk to a corner away from Bob when he came in the door. Bob opened the back door and ushered Streak into the yard for the night. Bob was too mentally exhausted to deal or punish Streak right now. He knew he was going to have him put to sleep, there was no question about that but not right now, he had more pressing issues on his mind, namely Ashley.

Bob couldn't sleep, he did not know what to do, except pray. Being Catholic and believing in the Virgin Mary, he began. "Virgin Mary, Mother of God please, please help my daughter keep her arm, Oh my God Please, Please Virgin Mother Help us." He prayed all night saying the Rosary, over and over again. He never counted how many times but he knew he was not going to stop until he had heard from the doctors in the morning. Again and again he recited the rosary asking for God's and the Virgin Mary help. Morning came and it found Bob still saying the Rosary. He was exhausted but he would not let himself fall asleep, never even closed his eyes to take a break from the intense praying.

The sun had been up a few hours and now it was almost time to call the hospital. Jan got up from her chair, where she had been sitting and praying along with Bob all night and started toward the phone. The hospital had answered and was getting the doctor to the phone for him. "Hi Bob, there's good news, we believe Ashley's arm will be all right the doctor reports. Bob falls back into a chair as his knees gave out. "It's the dandiest thing, yesterday that arm did not have a 20% chance of recovering and now this morning it has already started to heal up really fine, quite the unusual case," the doctor says. Bob burst out in tears of joy. "Thank you Virgin Mother, thank you, thank you for saving my daughter's arm," and continues to weep. "Prayer, aye Bob?, That's wonderful," the doctor tells him. "Yes, prayer has worked on more than one on ofmy patients in the past, I'm glad it worked for you." Bob, through his tears thanked the doctor and said they would be there soon.

The weight of the dark cloud had lifted and Bob was filled with gratitude and joy. He couldn't thank Mary enough for answering his prayers. Knowing Ashley was well-taken care of now, he decides to stop and buy a dozen of long stem white roses and leave them at the shrine to The Virgin Mary at his church before going to the hospital. Knowing that, without Her help, Ashley's would not have had a chance of keeping her arm after such an attack. Arriving at the hospital he met his daughter beaming with satisfaction that she would be keeping her arm. Bob and Jan comforted Ashley as best they could with their reassurance that she would be all right.

With Ashley in the hospital for a few days' Bob had the disparaging job of taking Streak to the Dog Pound to be put to sleep. Bob knew he could do nothing else. He absolutely did not want the dog in his home or in anyone else's and felt it was the safest thing for everyone's protection. He hardly gave thought that he had spent months and hundreds of dollars attack training Streak. All he could do is thank God and the Virgin Mary for their intercession in helping Ashley. To this very day, Bob buys, once a month, a dozen long stemmed white roses for the Virgin Mary's shrine at his church.

The End

CHAPTER 4

▼

THE CHASE

Here it is a Saturday night, with five 19 year old young men in need of something to do and desperate to find it. Jack, Al, Dick, Dave and I had been cruising around in Jack's car to all the hot spots in town but nothing special was happening. "Let's go to the cemetery," Jack says. "Yea, let's go. We haven't been there in months.", Dave replies. "Yea let's go," Al ads. We all agreed and headed toward the cemetery.

This cemetery was not an ordinary cemetery. This cemetery was very old. It dated back to the Civil War Days of the United States. It was about ten miles away and on a small hill, a dirt road the only way in and out of it. When we got on the dirt road, Jack started showing off his driving skills, spinning the tires and fish tailing from one side of the road to the other, throwing dust and dirt everywhere. About a 1/4 mile in, we stopped at the side of the road by the old cyclone fence. We all got out of the car and jumped the fence running up the hill into the cemetery. Once in the heart of the cemetery we started chasing each other around the head stones, yelling and acting like a bunch of adolescent fools. After a half an hour of this wild exertion we decide to leave before someone called the police on us. The nearest house was a 1/4 of a mile away but they could have heard our loud caring on. We carried on our foolishness all the through the cemetery, down the hill and back over the fence to the car. We all piled back into the car and slowly started rolling down the dirt road through the darkness toward the main highway continuing to be loud and cocky.

Jack's Plymouth had bucket seats and there were five of us. We sat two in the front and three in the back. I had the middle seat in the back between Dick and Al, with Dave sitting shotgun and Jack driving. As we were rolling down the road, I happen to look at the rear view mirror, that was directly in front of me at the windshield. I looked, blinked, and looked again. I could not believe what I was seeing. Not trusting what I saw in the mirror, I turned around in the seat and looked out the rear window of the car. With my mouth hanging open in disbelief, I turned back and sat facing forward, looking into the mirror, still seeing what I had seen the first time and still not believing it.

"Jack, look in the rear view mirror," I said. The other guys were still being rowdy and paid no attention to me. Jack looked in the mirror, gazed at it for a moment, then turned around in his seat to look out the rear window, then spun back to look in the mirror again and floored it, pedal to the metal, the car took off and we were flying down the road, dust and dirt coming off those tires like no tomorrow.

Jack and I both kept our eyes on the rear view mirror, hardly believing what we were seeing. We were gaining, more and more distance on them, what a relief. Not a word was spoken between Jack and I. It happened so fast that the other guys in the car had not known what we had just seen. Eventually what we had seen disappeared into the flying dust of the road trailing off the back of the speeding car. What did we see? What was gaining on us? It may be hard to believe but it was two men with long handle bar mustaches, wearing Civil War Days long duster coats, knee high boots and cowboy hats. That's what! They were chasing after the car as hard as they could with their arms swinging and unbuttoned coats flying in the breeze. We had seen them in the mirror but could not see them out the back window of the car. That's what had startled us. For fear of being razed about it, Jack or myself ever said a word to them about what we had seen that night.

That night's experience is something Jack or I will ever forget. There was no doubt about it, we had seen some real ghosts that had truly scared us. Jack and I became believers that night. That was the last time we went fooling around at that or any cemetery ever again. That sighting was definitely enough to convince us that the spirit world truly exists. Feeling lucky to get away that time, not knowing what would have happened if they had caught up to the car, we felt there was no need to ever act so high handed around a cemetery again. To see such a thing is not believing, it's really knowing.

The End

CHAPTER 5

▼

OUT OF THE BLUE
AND
INTO THE PINK

I was raised with 12 years of Catholic schooling. Read a bit about eastern religions, Hinduism Yogis, Monks, ECT…but I always prayed to the Virgin Mary, Jesus and some Saints, even in my Harley riding days of 25 years. You know those little miracles that happen where things just work out for you. That's one thing, but this happening was something else. I worked for my brother delivering homemade pie's in Phoenix, Arizona. I delivered them to restaurants all over the city, from greasy truck stops to high class resorts. I started at 3:00 a.m. and was done by 1 p.m. Some three hundred pies were delivered each day.

One day, I had a list from a manager of a Big Boy restaurant. It was a special order for his son's birthday party. Delivery was to be about 12:00 P.M. at his restaurant. I picked up that order along with all the others that morning from the factory that made the pie's in downtown. All day long, hour after hour, this order, that was written on a pink piece of paper, lay on the inside motor cover of the delivery step-van I was driving. At a restaurant, the stop just before the Big Boy, as I left the driveway, I saw the pink note on the motor cover. Once I got there, it would be only a short time before I could call it a day and go home.

When I got to the Big Boy, a distance of about 3 miles, I looked at the motor cover and the note was gone. I wondered where could it have gone? I parked the truck and looked all around, on the floor in the front of the truck, on the floor in the back of the truck, under the pie racks. I looked in the parking lot and under the truck but the special order on the pink piece of paper was nowhere to be seen.

I was panicking. I was 23 years old and my brother was 33 and big. He never had physically hurt me, but he could be scary with his size and temper. I put the truck back into gear, went down the driveway of the Big Boy and headed back toward the restaurant I had just came from because I know I had last seen it there. As I drove up the driveway, I was looking around the parking lot but didn't see the note. I parked, got out of the truck and looked some more. I still did not find it. I got back into the truck and started to drive back to the Big Boys' restaurant up the road. I was starting to get scared. Just the fear of explaining to my brother what had happened to the list of pie's to be dropped off was enough to make me sweat. I began to pray to Saint Anthony, Patron Saint of lost articles. "Saint Anthony can you help me find this pink piece of paper?" "My brother is going to kill me for losing it."

All of a sudden, at that same moment, everything started to turn black from the outside of my peripheral vision and it was closing in fast. The truck was still rolling but I wasn't thinking about it. All I could see like a light at the end of a long tunnel, a small spot of sight was the only thing left as I looked down the road. Then my head turned to the right, without me moving it on my own. My view was a plowed field through this small circle of vision. My head stopped and my eyes focused, there was the pink piece of paper. It was like I was standing right over it and seeing it clearly. It was just a few feet from it.

Then, SNAP, I was back behind the wheel of the rolling truck, with a full field of vision. I hit the brakes, put the truck in neutral and set the parking brake. Then I got out and looked at this field about 5 acres in size. There was something out there, about 75 yards away. As I walked across this field, step by step, I could see that there was something pink there all right. It was! It was the pink piece of paper. I was flabbergasted, not knowing what to think. Sure enough, as I walked up to it, I saw that it was the pink note I had lost. I bent down and picked it up, hardly believing my eyes. It was like being in the "Twilight Zone."

This was, to me, something that the word miracle does not even come close to describing. My Faith had been confirmed, I looked toward the heavens and thanked St. Anthony for his favor of helping me. It was so moving that it even happened. It was truly an outstanding experience. Like I said, small miracles happen all the time to people but this was something else.

The End

CHAPTER 6

THE VIRGIN
AND
THE BIKER

I've got to get out of here! It's 4:00 a.m. and I was running late for work. Had spent the night at my girlfriends and now had a fifteen-mile ride ahead of me to get home, change my clothes and get to work on time. I had only just started this new job two weeks ago and really needed to keep it.

Rolling out of bed and putting my clothes on, I was worried about getting to work on time. Barely running a comb through my hair, I headed for the front door with an unbuttoned shirt. The morning air was crisp, clear with the stars still shining brightly against the still dark sky. Zipping up my leather jacket and swinging a leg over my Harley, I gave it a few good kicks and it started. Idling for just a short while, I put it in first gear and headed out of the yard, down the drive, into the street and toward the Expressway.

Once I got onto the Expressway I turned that throttle up, I did not have time to waste. Traffic was light but slowly building with pick up trucks of construction workers who usually started at dawn. I was clipping right along with only the tail lights of two vehicles in sight, which were about an eighth of a mile ahead of me, One in my far right lane and one in the center lane further ahead. Behind me, I could see in my mirror, there were about four cars a quarter of a mile back. I was coming up to a part of the Expressway in the city that did not have any lighting along it. With tall bushes on each side, you couldn't even see the lights of the oncoming traffic. The sun had still not dawned, so it was as dark as midnight at this part of the road.

Things can get a bit scary at times when riding 500 pounds of metal at a good rate of speed. Even for myself, with more than twenty years of Harley Motorcycle riding experience, the fear of having a serious accident at anyone moment, tends to command respect for life itself. As in the past, any time I got a little worried while riding, I prayed to the Virgin Mary for Her protection. So this night, I had done the exact same thing as I came to this dark part of the Expressway. On top of just waking up and being worried about showing up for work on time, I prayed to the Virgin Mary for a safe ride home. Prayer completed, I rolled into this darkness at 70 miles an hour. All of a sudden from out of no where, for lack of a better or more accurate description, this dark black cloud appeared ahead and above me and was floating toward me. I could see it coming. It just came from in front of me and swung around to my right side and came to me. It wasn't like it was in me, it was like I was in it. I was surrounded by a warm black velvet presence. I could almost see what it was. It seemed to be a big bearded man, with long black hair blowing in the wind. His leather jacket and pants were shining in the darkness of the night. He was all around every part, but I don't think I could see the leather and Levi's on my own arms and legs, only his. Then I noticed that the sky had turned a deeper royal blue and the stars were twinkling much brighter. It was as though the haze of the city lights and pollution in the air had totally, disappeared. I could not feel the vibrations of the bike or the wind in my face any more and on top of that, he was steering and in total control. Without having any idea what was happening, the bike leaned and changed lanes to the left, smoothly, quickly and with determination, without so much of a thought or muscle movement from me.

Before I knew it, a large piece of plastic, large enough to cover a car, went flying by on my right-hand side. I would have been covered with it and surely would have lost control of the Harley and crashed. Just as it passed, I, I mean, we and the bike, under his control, changed back to the right lane, again not checking for traffic, at least I didn't look. There was no time, I was still in awe of what was happening. As we got into the right lane, four to six, wooden 2x4's went flying past us in a tangled, tumbling array in the middle lane from the back of a second pick up truck in that lane that was just ahead of us. It all happened so fast. Like on an amusement ride that throws your body in unpredict-able directions any unpredictable moment. You are at its mercy with-out a clue as to the next move. This is as near a description as I can describe.

Without any warning, I was back by myself, alone on the bike. In the wink of an eye, the big biker spirit had vanished. At that instant, I felt the bike with all it's vibration, the wind in my face and I could see my hands on the handle bar grips again. The sky and stars had turned dim and hazy again, as they were before he appeared. The tail lights of those vehicles were still in front of me as I began to wonder what had happened.

I wasn't shook up, it was as though I had just woken up from a dream very relaxed, but I wasn't in bed, I was on my Harley, rolling at 70 mph. I thought to myself, did that really happen? Was I dreaming? Am I going crazy? I had no quick explanation. I thought about turning around to look for the plastic and 2x4's but then I thought and remembered the prayer. I concluded to think that I had just been saved from a horrible fate of a terrible accident by the Virgin Mary. Right then and there I just decided to believe that it was divine intervention and that was that. I continued down the highway toward home, never looking back. I thanked The Virgin Mary for Her and the spirits, my guardian angels, for this is whom I believed had been driving the bike, protection. I am filled with excitement and awe realizing that I have seen the power of God at work first hand. This is something that I can never forget. Nor can I ever disbelieve in the existence of the Virgin Mary, God or any of his servants, from now until forever. For it was shown to me, they are there, without a doubt, very real, very beautiful and very powerful. Seeing is not believing, for me, it's knowing.

The End

CHAPTER 7

▼

LIKE A LEAF IN THE BREEZE

Saturday 6:00 A.M. What in the world would a hard-working man get up for, so early, on his day off? To ride his Harley Motorcycle with hundreds of others in a helmet protest. That's what. Starting from downtown Detroit to a city park all the way on the west side of town. Somehow I have a lot of energy this morning, unlike most work days. A few cups of coffee and I'm outside warming up the bike. I can hear Jim coming up the street, pipes roaring. He must have gotten up real early to be here already. I love when a plan comes together. Jim says he's already had four cups of coffee and is ready to roll. I give him the thumbs up, lock the door, jump on my bike and roll down the driveway toward the street.

It was a perfect day, high of 85 degrees with clear blue skies. We made it downtown in 20 minutes. In the canyon of all these tall building with their steel, concrete and glass with the pipes of our motors echoing off it all, was always a moving experience. Last year there were 500 riders that met for this run but more than that was expected this year. We had arrived early at the center square. There were only about 50 other bikes there then. As time went by we could hear more and more the distant thunder of bikes filling up the out of view side streets, around downtown.

Departure time arrived and the bikes started to roll out of downtown. Our group, from around the town square, had to wait about a half an hour before we had the room to start rolling. Spectators lined the streets to see the endless supply of motorcycles and riders parade past them. Once on the expressway we could not see the front of the pack. It looked as though one was looking at a long serpent winding over the small hills and curves ahead. Final count, we learned later, was 3,000 motorcycles. What a grand turn out it had become.

After about an hour of riding we arrived at the park. It was a mad house. A nice big party, races over here, contests over there and plenty of motorcycles and girls to gawk at. The beer was flowing and everyone was having a good time. Hours of Harley talk, running across old friends and making new ones. These are my kind of people. It wasn't long though before the sun was starting to set and it was time to go. We all promised each other to make the run next year and bid each other Happy Trails.

Jim and I were on the way home, rolling through the park toward the expressway that would bring us back to our own neighborhood. When we got on the entrance ramp, we began to gain speed. 50, 60, 70 mph as we entered the expressway lanes. It seemed like there was no reason in the world to settle in at this speed because the road was clear for as far as we could see, so we didn't. 80, 90,100 mph. At that speed everything is vibrating so much along with the wind in your face, your vision becomes blurred. I was to the left of the far left high speed lane of the freeway. Jim was to my right in the same lane.

Having a newer model Harley with a stronger engine, Jim began to pull ahead of me. I was up to 105 mph, really blurry now but I can make out Jim just ahead of me on my right by a few feet. Before I knew what was happening I realized I was directly behind Jim's bike. My front tire just missing his rear tire by about a foot and still drifting to the right. I crossed the line into the next lane and still was still drifting into the lane to the right of me. I had no control. I backed off the throttle. When the bike got to the dividing line, between the first and second lanes to my right, it threw itself back to the left crossing both lanes again. When it got to the solid white line of the shoulder, the bike threw itself back to the right back across the lanes again. Again and again I was being hurled across the two lanes of the Expressway at break neck speeds. Again and again, back and forth, back and forth I went. I was in a high speed wobble, at more than 100 mph, like a leaf in the breeze that's still connected to the branch, flipping violently to and fro in a desperate attempt to hang onto the branch, faster that one can count it swings from one side to the other. That's how I felt, like a leaf in the breeze, a 100 mph breeze.

Amazingly enough, I was still up on my two wheels. The foot pegs must have just been missing the pavement, I dared not look. When the bike changed directions it would be leaning at a 45-degree angle so I knew they had to be close. Because I had let off the throttle, I began to slow, 80 mph, I knew I was slowing down but still being hurled back and forth at a rapid pace across the lanes. I was now covering a lane and a half, back and forth, back and forth. At 60 mph, I was down to covering one lane, from line to line. I had been in a 60 mph high speed wobble before so I knew there is absolutely nothing one can do, except let off the throttle, hang on and pray that you can ride it out. You don't dare raise your foot to apply the brakes because it throws the gyro motion and balance of the bike off by shifting the weight. Nothing to do but sit tight and hope you stay up on two wheels.

Half a lane, back and forth, back and forth, still one does not have the strength to stop the gyro inertia of the 600 pounds of motorcycle and rider. 40 mph, covering less that a ½ of the lane. At 25 mph I was covering a 1/4 of the lane. Daring to raise my leg, I tapped the brake and shifted down to second gear. I finally had gained control. Still up on two wheels, alive and in one piece. Today was not the day that I was to be made into road hamburger. That was a relief. Before throttling back up, I remember glancing back. There, ten car lengths behind me were three cars, one in each of the lanes of the expressway. They were holding back all the traffic behind them so they would not run over me if I crashed. They must have seen the whole wild ride I had just taken. At 100 mph. I covered one mile in 36 seconds and this ride seemed to last an hour. I thought, will that be a scary story to tell the Grand Kids, theirs and mine

Jim was nowhere in sight. I throttled up, back to high way speed, 70 mph. I didn't worry about the wobble coming back at that speed. I knew it would only kick in at more than 100 mph. Soon I saw Jim on the side of the expressway looking back over his shoulder for me. He pulled out and met me in my lane. "What happened?" He yelled over the roar of the bikes. "Awe nothing." I yelled back at him. He shrugged his shoulders and we continued our ride home. I couldn't help but feel like a very lucky man living through such an experience. Who or what had kept me from becoming a permanent part of the road was a mystery to me. I was just grateful that it didn't happen or I would have been writing this story with a stick in my mouth from a wheel chair, if I had been even that lucky.

The End

CHAPTER 8

▼

PEOPLE UNDER GLASS

Saturday night and time to Rock 'n Roll. I had started a new job two weeks ago and had received my first pay check today. I planned this night out for a week, a night to remember. I was headed downtown to a very popular night club. Downtown in a big city can be a strange place for a boy from the suburbs. I was about to travel through streets with poor street lighting, boarded up buildings with lots of neighborhood street people hanging out on every corner. I had to watch out for myself, I thought, as I began the drive to the club.

Leaving my suburb, I crossed over the line dividing the two cities. One can see the very visible change in the surroundings. The buildings, with their peeling paint and unkept landscaping. The litter also was very evident along with the dress of the people. About half way there it had begun to rain. This made it even a little more frightening with the threat of becoming involved in an accident in this part of town. I put on the windshield wipers as I noticed the traffic light up ahead had turned red. I slowed as I came to it and stopped at the red light. I was the first one in the lane at the crosswalk line. As I waited for the light to turn green, I bent over and started to put a tape into the tape player. From that angle, I glanced up, and saw the light to be green. At that moment, I sat up straight and pushed on the gas petal, not wanting to hear the sound of a horn of an impatient driver behind me, not in this neighborhood.

SSSSSCREACH!!! I had just rolled a couple of feet into the cross street when I had heard this awfully loud screeching of tires. I cringed, as one often does when you hear tires screeching and do not know exactly what direction the sound is coming from. All you can do is wait for the collision and hope it is not with you. I braked to a stop. When the screeching had stopped, I looked up. A white Cadillac was passing in front of me in the cross street blowing his horn as he went by the front end of my car. You S.O.B., you could have killed someone running a red light like that, I remember saying to myself. Just at that moment I noticed the traffic light was red for me and green for the cross traffic. What the Hell? I thought I had just seen it green for me. No, I must have been mistaken. I actually had just ran a completely red light and pulled out into cross traffic. Oh Brother, I thought, glad that Cadillac didn't hit me, I would have been knocked into next Tuesday with an impact from that big car. About that time I had noticed that there was something big just outside my drivers side window. I looked but couldn't quite make it out what it was. It was about two feet off the ground and it was shinny, like the water on the black top road, but what was it? Then I realized it was chrome. It was a bumper, a bumper of a full size City Bus. It was so close that I could have reached out my driver's window and touched it. That's where the screeching had come from, I thought. The driver had slammed on the brakes and skid to within two feet of my car door. I was speechless and grateful it had stopped in time.

As I looked up to the large windshield of the bus, I saw people, people that were pressed up against the windshield, three deep. They must have been standing in the isle of the bus and when the driver hit the brakes and they were hurled forward up against the glass. Little old ladies and little old men pressed against the glass with their contorted faces, just like a kid make faces on a window. They were being held there as the other passengers tried to gain their balance, to get off of them. I knew instantly I was in big trouble. I had run a red light into oncoming traffic. I panicked, and looked straight ahead, the cross traffic had cleared and the light had turned green for me now. I stepped on the gas to get out of the intersection. As I started moving, I decided at that instant that I would just keep right on rolling. It was wrong but I was too scared to do anything else. I was watching my rear view mirror for police over the next couple of miles. It had been like a dream, a bad one. I got to the club and ordered one stiff drink to calm my nerves. Well, it sure turned out to be a night to remember, after all and I had lived through it.

That following Monday, I had gone into work still thinking about what had happened two nights earlier, hoping the passengers on that bus were O.K. After punching in at the time clock, I walked up to the group of fellow workers by the coffee machine. As I got closer, I heard one guy talking about a bus accident he had seen over the weekend. "Yea, that bronze colored Monte Carlo pulled right out in front of that bus. Lucky for him that driver stopped in time, he would have been dead from the impact." I felt faint. It was me he was talking about. "Nobody was seriously hurt on the bus. It just scared everyone." Then, I don' t know why, but I blurted out, "That was me!" The group all turned and looked at me. The same guy asked, "That was you?" "Yea," I said as I hung my head. "I swore that light had turned green for me." The guy asked me the same question again in disbelief. "That was you?", "man you sure got lucky that the bus did not smash into you." He said as they all stood there with their expressions and comments of disbelief. I couldn't help but think, that now it would be a night to remember for all of them, too. What luck, to have had a co-worker see the whole hair-raising scene. I can't believe, that all I wanted to do was to have a good time down in the city.

The End

CHAPTER 9

▼

SAFE

Today was the day. I was getting transferred to a new department at the shop. It had been a year since I put the application in and today was the day I started in the Inspection Department. At long last I would have an easy, clean job with some dignity. Quite a change from working in the bowels of the plant, with all the other factory rats' I had worked with side by side for more than 10 years. I was on top of the world, as I rode to work on my motorcycle, clipping through the city streets toward the plant. It was a beautiful summer day that was making my mood even better. I really felt like somebody and that nothing could go wrong.

It didn't take long though for that illusion to fade away. I rounded a corner, three blocks from the plant, in a warehouse area. The road ahead was clear, so I opened it up a little more. 60 m.p.h. and the motor was just purring. When all of a sudden, out of an alleyway, the rear of a trailer of a semi truck appeared. I didn't have time to stop. I didn't have time to do much, the collision was emanate. I locked up the brakes and began to skid. I was sliding right for the side of the trailer. I guess it was instinct but all I could think of to do, at this point, was to lay the bike down, so I did. Slamming the bike to the ground on the left side I could hear metal scrapping the pavement as I slid.

Amazingly my left leg and knee were not touching the ground because of the front and rear foot pegs. I realized next, I was sliding under the trailer, right between the front and rear tires and it was still rolling out of the alley. I saw the undercarriage of the trailer, as I was sliding under it. I could almost have counted the rivets and bolts because it seemed like an eternity but had actually been just a matter of seconds. I had slid clear from under the trailer and was still sliding on the pavement, when by chance, I tapped the handle for the front brake. To my amazement, the bike stood up on it's two wheels. The front tire had grabbed just enough to stand the bike up on it's two wheels. I was up and rolling down the road again, in one piece. I didn't feel any pain or discomfort, see any blood nor did I feel shaken by the incident, it had happened so fast. I could not believe it. I was back in control, and doing just fine.

Two blocks to go and I felt on top of the world again. I pulled up to the guard shack, where us workers parked our motorcycles. I stopped, turned off the ignition and put the kickstand down into position. Leaned the bike onto the kickstand and swung my right leg over the seat to get off. The next thing I know was that I was on the ground. My knees had given out, they were weak and trembling. I managed to stagger to a standing position while holding onto the bike for balance. The guard came running up to me from his guard shack. "You O.K. man? He asked. "Oh yea, just another day at the office." I replied.

The End

CHAPTER 10

THE SLIDE

What a beautiful day! The clouds have moved out and the sun is shining bright. The car is loaded, with as much as one can load into the trunk and onto the roof of Volkswagen car. It was warmed up and ready to go. I was heading for California in the dead of a Michigan winter. Just can't take this frigid weather anymore. I have planned this move and now I am executing it. I said good-byes to all my friends and family, who wished they could come along, over the past week. I'm leaving Michigan driving South through Indiana toward Oklahoma and straight west to California.

The roads were a little snow covered all the way through Indiana but the snow was getting heavier. By the time I got to St. Louis the roads became icy with about a foot of snow on top of it and still coming down. I decided to take a well-deserved rest, get a bite to eat and some hot coffee to warm me up. These VW heaters are not the best in the world in these cars. I got through the doors of the restaurant. It felt so good to be totally surrounded by the warmth. I just stood there a moment absorbing the heat while unzipping my coat. Spotting an open table, I walked over and sat down at it. The waitress was headed my way and I was ready to order. "Hi, ready to order?" she asked, "You bet! Coffee and the special please"; I replied. "O.K. you got it. By the way, which way are you headed?" She asked. "West to California, "I can't wait to feel that warm weather," I said with a smile on my face. "Well," she said, "there's a girl over there hitchhiking to Arizona if you want a passenger?" "Over there the girl with the blue jacket on." I looked over in the direction the waitress was pointing. Wow, not bad, I said to myself. "Sure tell her to come over," I told the waitress. "O.K." she said as she walked away, "I'll tell her."

Long curly blond hair, nice fitting blue jeans, about 25 years old, no wedding ring and here she comes toting along a small suite case. The only room for anything was in the front and back seats, I left it that way in case I had to sleep in the car. So the suite case would fit. "Hi, how you doing?" I say. "Fine, except for a West bound ride." She says.

"Well I'm going West and you can ride with me if you want?" I say. "Sure, sounds good." Going to see my mother in Arizona." She replies. "I'll be passing right through Arizona on my way to California," I respond." "Lets eat and hit the road before we loose too much daylight, sound good?", I ask. "Yea," she agrees.

The VW was still a little warm when we got back to it. Suitcase went into the back, she got in the front seat and off we went down the ice and snow-covered road. All of a sudden, as we got around a curve, I could see cars slowing down and 10 or 12 cars pulled off on the side of the road. Probably an accident, I thought to myself, but as we got closer we could see that the cars on the side of the road were just parked with their occupants looking down a hill of the road just ahead. We decided to stop and take a look what the attraction was. Sure thing, it's a steep hill all right. We could see cars and trucks in the snow banked shoulders of the road where they had slid off the roadway and had gotten stuck. "All you have to do is go down this hill to the top of the next one and down again, then the road levels out and you home free from there," said a man who was standing in the crowd. Most of the cars we could see were making it down and up the other side. I didn't think it would be that difficult. So we got back into the VW and started moving for the drop off of the hill.

Over the edge we went, 30, 40, 50 m.p.h. The road was icy here so I dared not hit the brakes, just holding on and keeping the old VW straight in the ruts as best I could. At 60 m.p.h., we had made it to the bottom and were on the way up the other hill. Yea, the tough part is over, I thought to myself. I put the petal to the metal as we climbed the incline. As we got closer to the top, we started to loose momentum. Oh no, we're not going to make the top, I was thinking as we slowed down. We were only 10 feet away from cresting the top when we started to slide backwards. "Oh no," she says, being terrified on the way down into complete silence, these were her first words after we had started down that hill. "Hold on," I said as I turned the wheel to the right so I would not back all the way down the hill. POOF, the snow when flying as the VW hit the embankment of snow at the shoulder. We didn't stop, we were still moving fast. We hit the safety fence on the other side of the shoulder and like a slingshot we were propelled forward from the tension of the fence, right through the path we just plowed while traveling backward. We came to a stop. I lifted my head. Incredibly the VW sat on the shoulder of the road only five feet from the top of the hill. Amazing, I thought, that we had not turned over or been stuck in the knee high snow any worse than we were.

The girl was crying, "Are you all right?" I asked. The crying continued. "I guess so, but I got so scared I wet my pants," she said. I didn't know what to say. I was thinking, however, that I'm not surprised that didn't happen to me. We got out of the VW. I surveyed the situation. We had about five feet of one foot high snow to dig out of from in front of the VW to get back on the road and we would be headed down the next hill to level ground.

"O.K.," I said to her, "I'll start digging the car out." "Why don't you go over to those trees and wash off a little?" Drying her tears she said, "O.K." In a little while I had the snow moved away from the front of the VW and she was headed back from the trees. "I'm Freezing," she says with a chattering voice. She did look a little blue. "Get in the back seat and wrap up in this wool blanket." I suggested. She crawled in and I wrapped her up with the blanket. I put the bottom of the blanket over the little heat vent on the floor so it would funnel the heat to her. "How's that, better?" I asked. "Yes, thank you," she shivered the reply. "I have a little more snow to move out from the front of the car and we'll be on our way again, don't you worry." I tried to reassure her, as she nodded her head in agreement.

I dug away the remaining snow and thought that with a little rocking of the car we could get free. I put the VW into gear, let off the clutch, foot on the gas, but the wheels were spinning in place. So I got out and pushed and rocked with my foot on the gas petal but to no avail. I couldn't rock it hard enough to break free. "Are you warm now?", I asked. "Yea, not too bad," she responded. "Well that's good because I'll need a little help to get this car out of here," I said. "What do you want me to do?" she asked. "I just need a little pushing on the back of the car so we can get the tires onto the road where they'll grab a little better," I tell her. "O.K." she says as she climbed from the comfort of the back seat and that warm blanket. She went around back and I got into position with my right foot on the gas petal and my left foot outside the car pushing and pulling on the door jam. Back and forth the VW rocked, "O.K., one more good push! Ready?" I yelled. There was no reply from her. Oomph, that did it we were getting free.

I jumped back in the VW as the tires caught some cleaner pavement. Now the tires were in the ruts of the road. The VW surged forward. I was at the top of the hill and still moving. All of a sudden I was going down the hill. We were free and headed in the right direction, at least. Faster and faster I swooped down the hill 30, 40 m.p.h. I remember thinking that she will have to walk down the hill to the car but there is nothing I could do about that now. I had my hands full keeping the VW on the road.

The road was leveling out and I could start to apply the brakes. Slower and slower I rolled while coming to a stop on the shoulder of the road. As I glanced in my rear view mirror, I saw people running toward the rear of the VW. They're all coming to congratulate me for making it down the hill in one piece, what a proud moment. As I stopped, I looked in the rear view mirror at the people milling around the rear of the car. What's wrong? I asked myself. Did the transmission fall out or something? I got out and walked to the back of the car, I couldn't believe my eyes. There was the girl laying face down in the road hanging onto the bumper, crying. What happened? She forget to let go? No. Her warm hands, having been bundled up in the blanket, stuck to the frigid bumper and consequently she had been dragged down the hill behind the VW. There she was laying face down, hair a mess, half covered with snow, hands stuck to the bumper and crying. I couldn't blame her, I might be crying too if I was in her situation.

Someone had brought over some water to pour on her hands to free them from the bumper. She stood up and started to shake the snow off herself. She wouldn't even look at me. She wasn't seriously hurt but shaken up quite a bit. I didn't know what to say, so I thought I would try to make her laugh about it. "Well, at least you didn't have to walk down the hill." Then she looked at me, with anger in her eyes. Being my joking self, I asked, "I guess marriage is out of the question?" The only reply was her angry stare. Guess it wasn't that funny after all.

The End

CHAPTER 11

ALL SHOOK UP

It was just another day slaving away in the auto factory. This was my ninety first day there. I was now an official member in the U.A.W...Full union protection and benefits. It was somewhat of a relief knowing I could not be fired easily with the Union's protection. I was a forklift driver in the press shop, a relief driver. My job was to take the place of another driver when they went on break, vacation, stayed home sick, or just stayed home.

There were 250 presses in this plant. They ranged from small ones that stamped out little clips and plates for various parts of cars to presses that with one downward motion, would press out the entire roof of a maxi-van. You could park a full size 1963 Cadillac in it sideways, fins and all. It rocked the floor when it came down. It stamped out a van roof every two minutes. There were 10 of these presses running all the time in this plant on the first floor.

This day they need me to fill in for a worker that didn't show up in the spot welding department on the second floor. I was to keep the hood line running. The spot welders, when the hod was complete, would load them vertically into a metal rack that measured 5 feet high, 6 feet wide and 12 feet long. They had 3 inch by 3 inch square tube rails at the ends and sides. The side rail came off, the hoods were slid in, 15 of them, and the rail locked back into place. I would pick up the rack with the fork lift, drive down the isle way and drop it off by the freight elevator that took it down stairs. There, other fork lift drivers that would pick them up and put them onto waiting box cars to be shipped to the assembly plant. My job also entailed supplying empty racks from the storage area to the line for them to load up with more hoods.

I met the foreman and he described the job to me. The racks would fill up pretty fast so I did not have time to dally around. The empty racks where stored down the isle way in the open space provided for them. They were stacked two high, four rows wide, in close vicinity of the workers so one had to be careful handling the racks. These racks could be stacked as high as you could balance them if you wanted to but there were strict limitations on stacking. Outside in the yard the where stacked up to five high, maximum safety heights allowed in the yard. The empty racks were stacked only two high inside for safety and because the clearance needed to stay under the girders of the building and what looked like sheet metal duct work hanging from the girders. There was only a six-inch clearance from the top rack to the duct work that ran above them. When I would lift the top rack off the bottom rack, it would bring the clearance from the duct work to the top of the top rack down to only three inches.

I had to drive like a madman to keep up with the demand of the line. Back and forth down the isle way. Grab an empty rack, race to the line, drop it, grab a full rack, race it to the elevator, drop it, race back, grab another empty rack and do it all over again, every 10 minutes through an eight-hour shift. One had to be a good fork lift driver to keep up and that's why they put me there, I was good.

One time, I was on my way to grab an empty rack. I pulled into the storage area with my forks up aimed for an upper rack. I drove the forks through the slots in the rack, lifted it and started backwards away from the bottom rack. All of a sudden the rack starts to slide off the forks of the truck. I stopped fast but when I did the rack jumped upwards, and caught on something. Before I knew what had happened, sparks were showering down on me like a hail storm. I cringed and put my head down to avoid the sparks. The fork lift was vibrating like blender for twenty seconds, which seemed like an hour. When the sparks had stopped showering down around me, I looked up. What had happened?, I asked myself.

I sat in the seat of the fork lift recuperating from the scare and vibration. I was pulling myself together when the next thing I realized was that there was no noise from the spot welding guns that were all around me. They had all stopped. I looked to my right. No guns were running. I looked to left. No guns were running. Now that's unusual, I thought. Have all of these people stopped working to see what had happened? Their going to get fired if they don' start back to work soon.

There was a total of 150 spot welders on this second floor and not one of them was working, the guns had all quit and the workers were all looking in my direction or at their spot welding guns trying to figure out why they had stopped.

A friend came running up and asks me if I'm all right. I say "Yea," and start to get off the fork lift. I was still vibrating. When my feet hit the floor my knees gave out and my friend caught me, held me up and walked me over to lean on a wall. Still, no one had started back to work. When these spot welding guns are running, it's a very loud work area but it was almost as silent as a church now.

I asked my friend, "What happened?" "You hit the main electric feed line to the welding guns." I looked up at the rectangle metal box above the racks and asked. "Those aren't the duct work for heat?" "No" He replies. "They're a compartment for the main electrical power lines to the spot welding guns." "The rack had caught a little inspection door on one and when it opened, the metal rack went inside and made contact with the uninsulated wire junction block." "Twenty Thousand volts of electricity had traveled through the rack to the fork truck." He explains. I replied. "No wonder it felt like I was riding a blender." The rubber seat and floor mat of the lift and the plastic of the steering wheel had insulated me from the onslaught of the voltage.

The foreman of the area and the Union Steward came up to me then to check to see if I was all right. I said yes, still feeling the vibrating in my body. The Steward said I had to go with him down stairs to the main office. On the way down the Steward told me I not only knocked out the second floor but also half of the first floor including the main offices, with its teletypes, phones and computers. "Great, just great," I replied. I knew what this walk meant. They were going to fire me. When we walked into the Plant Superintendent's Office, they're where two uniformed factory guards there. I knew what it was about now, they were going to fire me for sure and the guards were there to escort me off the plant grounds. It was standard practice for them to do this.

I had to think fast and knew exactly what I was going to say to the plant Superintendent. I saw the Superintendent bent over the desk filling out my discharge papers. The Steward spoke up first, "You wanted to see this man, John?" We knew why we were there but there was a procedure of language that had to be said for the record. "I'm firing him," the Superintendent said. "For what John?" the Steward asked. "For shutting down production for twenty minutes." Just then the foreman of the area where I had been working comes into the office. "John, we only lost ten minutes of production, the workers took their ten minute break when it went down." "Im still firing him" the Superintendent replied. The Steward said something about taking it easy on me because I was a new employee. The Superintendent just sat there, still filling out the paper work when I decided to speak up. "It's a good thing I didn't die." The Superintendent had stopped writing, I had gotten his attention. I continued, "Because my parents would have ended up being rich people." "With all of the electricity, there are no warning signs on that electrical compartment."

The Superintendent said, Well, you should have been more careful, I'm going to give you three months off without pay." Immediately I said, "Yea, I think O.S.H.A.," the Federal Occupational Safety and Health Administration, "would like to know about the company forcing us to stack those racks in there two high with only inches of clearance from all that electricity." The Superintendent drops his pen on the desk and looks at me for the first time and says. "O.K., I'll give you only three days off." I looked at the Steward and asked. "Do you have the phone number to O.S.H.A. on you?" The Superintendent says. "O.K., O.K., I'm sending you home for the rest of the day, the next three hours of your shift." I looked at him and said. "O.K., but with pay." The Superintendent looked at his desk and then shook his head and replied 'Yea, O.K." He had given up. When we walked out of the office, the Steward had a big smile on his face and said, 'You got him, you got him good," and asked, "You ever consider running for a Union

Steward?" I just looked at him, grinned and said, "I have my own problems to deal with." We laughed in unison.

The End

CHAPTER 12

▼

CHOO CHEW

Look at me, kicked back and driving this brand new Dodge automobile hot off the assembly line. Man is this cool. It looks so good. It has a jet-black paint job, fully loaded plush interior, whitewalls, custom hub caps, man, I'm styling big time. I could see all the eyes upon me as I rolled this beauty down the road, I was just brimming with pride.

O.K. time to come back to reality. Making the turn into the driveway and into the parking lot, I searched for an open space. Parked the car, got out, slammed the door and headed for the pick up van. I had to keep reminding myself that it was only a job. The car was not mine. It belonged to the Chrysler Corporation. I was a driver on the night shift at the factory. As drivers, we drove the new cars from the plant to parking lots, a few blocks away. There they were loaded onto semi truck car hauling trailers and being transported to dealerships all over the country. I was a new hire in the first week of employment, so the excitement of driving these beauty's was quite a thrill. They all gleamed from the paint to the chrome, drove smoothly, sounded good and of course smelled like the new cars that they were.

The road to the lot was a wide two lane black top road. The street lights were dim in this industrial area of factories and steel mills. The buildings that were not operating at night were dark and seemed like shadows on the side of the road. When it rained the black top glistened throwing reflections in all directions. People crossing the street could hardly be recognized as human, as they melted in so well with the darkness and shadows. After leaving the plant and about a half block away there was a set of two rail road tracts running across the road. On these tracts, trains brought materials and parts to factories in the area. There were no gates on these tracts to stop oncoming traffic. In the day time a rail worker would stand in the road with a red flag to warn traffic of an approaching train. At night a rail worker would stand on the front of the engine and hold a dimly lit red railroad lantern out in front of him as it rolled at about 25 miles per hour across the road way. There was a lot less traffic at night, so they didn't bother getting in the roadway. There was of course a large single light near the top of the locomotive's engine but it is not easy to see from road level being near 15 feet from the ground and aimed far down the tracts.

One night as I drove from the plant toward the lot to park a car, I was approaching the tracts. It was a rainy night and I had the windows up. Radio going and feeling like a kid with a new car and that nothing could go wrong, I reached the railroad tracts. I slowed as before and looked in both directions for oncoming trains. We didn't encounter them very often so a glance was all that usually took place. Not seeing one I kept rolling and started across the tracts.

Suddenly the car shook from an impact and turned 90 degrees to the right. The car was shaking violently, the window broke and there was an awful sound of metal crunching and being torn apart as I was bounced around the interior. The car had been struck by a slow-moving train and was being dragged, entangled with the side of the loco-motive, down the tracts. When I had realized what had happened I reached for the passengers' door, opened it and jumped out, landing on my feet but soon ending up on my back in the mud. The crunching could still be heard as I stood up shaking from the shock of it all. I was standing within 12 feet of this, all black, very large, piece of machinery, rumbling and shaking the ground as it rolled by me down the tracts. The car, still attached to the train by its left side, was dancing around in a very erratic manner as it was being dragged down the tracts into the darkness. I could see the tail light on the right side jumping around like a sparkler in the hands of an excited child on the Forth of July.

I could not believe I had not seen it coming down the tracts as I had started to cross them. With the windows closed, covered with rain and the head light of the train being so high, I did not see it. On top of that there had been no railroad worker on the front of the engine with a lantern, it was raining too hard for him to stand out there. I had actu-ally run right into the side of the engine right at the front of it.

The train had finally stopped and by then the other drivers that were following me where at my side asking me if I was all right. Shaken but unhurt, except for my pride, we went to inspect the entangled train and car. The car was half eaten up, like it had been chewed on by a large beast, come to think of, it had. The car had been torn open from the front to the rear on its left side. Bumpers sticking out in an ugly fashion, side, front and rear windows shattered and the hood bent in half and aiming at the night sky. "Oh boy, this was a good one," a fellow driver commented as we surveyed the damage. "Your damn lucky to have gotten out of this one alive," another says. Yes that's exactly how I felt and then some. I also thought I was really lucky that I was not another 10 or 15 feet farther onto those tracts. I would have been struck by the front of that engine right in the driver's door with no means of escape as it was pushed down the tracts. I was lucky to survive this accident. Too bad I couldn't say the same for the car.

I was able to keep my job, thanks to the Union that fought for me, because the rail workers were held at fault for not having a man either on the road or on the front of the engine to warn or stop traffic. I was lucky again with that decision. I was given a job inside the plant as a repairman, which was all right with me. The incident had made me a little gun shy of driving cars across railroad tracts for some time.

The End

CHAPTER 13

WESTBOUND

Well. My plans are set. I'm going west to Arizona. I've had enough of this cold weather and the daily misery that it brings. Snow shoveling, ice scraping, dressing like an Eskimo, wet, cold, I can't take it any more. I'm out of here in a month. That's the plan. Get my belongings together, get the trailer uncovered and load it up. Everything is going with me. Motorcycle, stereo, some furniture, everything I can fit in either the van or trailer. I do not plan to come back for anything. I had accomplished this in two weeks, gave my notice at work and planned a going away party for next weekend. Yea, that's for me. Warm weather, sunshine, what a life to look forward to. I couldn't wait to get there.

The week went by fast and it was now time to party. There were going to be lots of friends I would be seeing for the last time or at least until they came out there to see me. Everyone showed up, to wish me a safe trip and to say their good byes. They all knew I wanted out of this weather. Some cried, some laughed but we all had a great time at the party. My best riding buddy, Ed, must have spent a fortune throwing this party, it was my leaving town gift.

I was leaving in two days. I was first headed to my parent's cottage up north, 80 miles away, to spend a few days with them before I left Michigan. I had pulled the van with the trailer connected out of the driveway and parked it in the street in front of the house. Borrowing a friend's car, I drove to the store to get some last minute supplies for the trip. On the way home, as I came up the street, I saw the van and trailer in front of the house. Why does the axle of the trailer look like that? I had owned this trailer for more than 10 years. It had hauled everything from motorcycles to bricks to furniture over the last 10 years. I guess it had gotten old and tired. I could see that the axle was bent. It had developed a bow to it. After all the weight I had loaded it for this trip and with its age, the axle had bent into a curve. It had to be changed or I would definitely not make it out of town let alone across the country with it like that.

Awe man, that means I have to unload it. What a bring down, and a postponement of the leaving date. I called the trailer shop that had built it for me 10 years earlier. The owner of the shop guaranteed that he could do it while it was loaded, but I had to wait four days for it to be done. Oh well, that's not too bad. My spirits were lifted in the relief of not having to unload and reload it again. The next morning I had towed the trailer to the shop. Dropping it off, the owner said he would do his best to get it done as soon as possible, two to four days. "O. K.," I said and thanked him for his efforts in advance. I figured I might as well work a few days to make the extra bucks instead of sitting around doing nothing while the trailer was repaired. I had gone back to driving a cab like I had done for the previous two years. In three days, I received the call that I could pick up the trailer at closing time the next day. All right, I'll be rolling westbound in no time. I had planned to go to my parents cottage right from the trailer shop. It was getting to be dusk when I picked up the trailer. Not bad, I thought, only an 80-mile drive, straight up the Interstate to the folk's cottage.

I should make good time, not much traffic out now. In fact, I had only seen three cars in the first 20 miles. About half way to the cottage I noticed something in the darkness off the right side of the expressway at the safety fence. It was a deer, a big eight point buck. I had thought how lucky I was to see such a large buck in the wild. My attention was drawn back to the road, checking my rear view mirrors for traffic. When I glanced back down the road in front of me, there was the buck, standing on the shoulder of the road with his right hoof on the white line of the first lane. I thought I'd better get out of this right-hand lane so I wouldn't hit him. I checked my left mirror for any traffic. It was clear and I started to change lanes immediately. When I looked back down the road in front of the van, there standing on the dividing line separating the lanes was the buck. He had walked out onto the expressway.

I'm traveling at 60 m.p.h. and the buck is now 40 to 50 feet directly in front of my van. A collision was inevitable. I braced myself, he lowered his head, then BAM, we made contact. His head fell from sight and the hood popped open. Blump, Blump, Blump, he had fallen to the ground and the wheels of the van and trailer had just rolled over him. I steered for the right side of the expressway, made it to the shoulder of the road and stopped. I remember thinking I did not see any steam coming from the radiator and felt joyed that there could not be that much damage. Jumping out of the van I left the motor running and headed straight back toward the deer that was now lying on the shoulder of the road about six or seven car lengths behind the van. When I had gotten to him I observed he was dead, not a breath left in his body as he lay motionless. I figured it was a quick and painless death for him at least. I grabbed the one antler left on his head and dragged him off the shoulder and into the grass. The other antler had been sheared off clean at the skull, nowhere to be found. I thought about gutting him right there and taking the meat but I had never even seen a deer being gutted before, so that was out of the question. I turned around and noticed the van. It was engulfed in what looked like smoke but was actually steam. I ran back to the van, reached in and shut the engine off. I walked around to the front of the van to inspect it. No, he didn't damage the radiator, he destroyed it. It was completely wrapped around the front of the engine with the grill holding it in place in a gnarled mess like a giant claw.

Oh great! Here I am on a lonely highway at night 40 miles from anywhere. Just great. Well, a State Trooper should be by eventually I figured, so I went and sat back in the van. Nothing else to do but wait. Soon, a set of yellow flashing lights were coming up the highway. It was a tow truck. I jumped out of the van and began waving like a madman. He pulled over with a car in tow. "I can call the station for you, and they'll send a truck out here," he said when I had gotten to his truck's side window. "O.K.," I replied. He called it in and said it wouldn't be long. I thanked him and he drove away.

It was thirty minutes before I saw another truck with his yellow flashing lights on coming up the highway. It pulled over and stopped in front of the van. "What happened," the driver asked as he got out of his tow truck. "I hit a deer, an eight-point buck that was crossing the highway," I replied. "Wow, you were lucky it didn't come through the windshield," he said. "Yea I know but with all the weight of a full van and trailer I hardly felt the impact." I replied. Then he asked me, "Where's the deer?" I walked him over to where it was. We discussed how it had been a waste of some good meat. Even the head for a trophy was ruined with the one antler broke off. We deciphered that the hide was still intact though and salvageable. I bargained with him, trading the deer for the tow to my parent's cottage. He accepted half price on the tow plus the deer. I agreed. I wasn't in much of a position to argue and he knew it.

We dragged the deer to his tow truck and wrestled its carcass onto the back of the it. Next, he hooked up to the van with the trailer behind and we were on our way. A few miles up the road I started to tell him about my trip west, the trailer axle being replaced and the delay it had caused me already. All of a sudden the motor of the tow truck began to sputter. "We got a problem," he blurted out and pulled over to the shoulder of the expressway. He got, out, opened the hood, climbed up on the bumper and started looking at the motor. "There's not much gas getting to the carburetor," he says on completing his inspection. "It's getting a little, so we should be able to roll slowly," he admitted. Gee! What a disappointment when I realized our top speed would only be 15 m.p.h., and we had 40 miles to go before we arrived at my parent's place. I asked myself, "What's next?" First a bent axle, an accident with an eight-point buck on the highway and now a forty-mile trip at 15 mph. I sat back in silence as we chugged up the road. Finally, nearly three hours later, we arrived at the cottage. Ma and Dad had been worried. I should have been there hours ago. Once they had heard what had happened and that I was all right, they relaxed. The tow truck driver left after unhooking the van and trailer. My parents and I went inside for the night.

The next morning I called my insurance company. They told me they would come and pick up the van and take it to a dealership 30 miles away to get fixed. I then called Ed back in the city, told him what had happened and asked him to pick me up. He agreed and said he would be leaving in a few minutes. On the way back he tried to cheer me up by saying that nobody wanted me to leave yet anyway and so he'll have another going away party for me. He also told me that if I didn't leave this time he'd take me himself. We laughed. I found out in the next few days that it would take three weeks before I could get the van back from the repair shop. The following weekend we had the second party. It was better than the first one. More friends showed up. Ed even hired the neighbor kid's band to play in the basement. The house was over flowing with people. They had spread to the front and back yards. Ten friends spent the night. They were too partied out to drive, so we partied until almost dawn with them.

I returned to work, at the cab company two days later while the van was being repaired. Three weeks later, Ed gave me a ride and I picked up the van from the shop up north and brought it back to the city. It was two days until the new departure date. I woke up the next morning and saw that it had started to snow. It was three days before it stopped. Twenty-eight inches had fallen in two days. A new record. I didn't believe it. I was two blocks from the westbound interstate expressway and the van and trailer are buried in snow, like every other car in town, with snow over the door knobs. The cab company wouldn't even let us try to take the cabs out. The snow had paralyzed the city. This was too much. I began to think that God did not want me to leave this city, ever. I drank and partied for the next three days while the city dug itself out one of worst snow storms in fifteen years. What timing! What would happen next?

It was Saturday. The snow had kept the city road crews busy but now they were clear to travel on. My friends talked me into one more party night with them and then they would let me leave on Sunday. I agreed, by now I was in no hurry, the wind had been knocked out of my sails for leaving by all that had happened over the last two months. We partied till late in the night. I woke up on a friend's couch, with the sun in my eyes coming in from the kitchen window. Everyone else was still asleep. I sat up, still in my clothes from the party. I stood up and headed for the kitchen to make a cup of coffee before I hit the road. As I walked toward the kitchen, I though it's best to be quiet so as not to wake anyone. They may keep me from leaving today, also. They were all great friends and meant well, but it was time to go.

As I got to the counter, looked out of the kitchen window. It was starting to snow again. A chill ran through my body. Awe man, not again! I started the coffee in a hurried fashion, spilling the grounds all over the counter. I couldn't get trapped here again. I ran to the couch, grabbed my jacket and went outside to warm up the van. I ran back inside and impatiently waited for the first cup to fill the coffee pot. I poured it into a cup and went to the front door of the house. I opened the door, stopped turned back and yelled, "Good bye, I'll drop you a postcard," then slammed the door, not waiting for a reply. I was determined that if I was only going to make it to the state line, I was still leaving. Now.

The roads were clear to the state line. As I drove into the night, the snow had turned to rain. The next morning it was still raining. I pushed on. Mile after mile, it rained as I crossed the country westbound. Four days later, I was in Arizona and the rain had stopped. The sun came out for the first time in a week. It felt and looked great. I finally could put a smile on my face knowing I had finally made it to the West.

BOOM, Plop, Plop, Plop. I looked into the right side mirror. Chunks of rubber were flying from the trailer tire. It was a blow out. I pulled to the side of the road and looked at the deflated tire. It was pretty much completely gone off the rim also. I didn't feel all that bad about it though. I had made it this far and this was nothing compared to the calamities I had endured. I changed the tire with a smile on my sun warmed face. It had been quite an experience but I had finally made it to the West!

The End

CHAPTER 14

OPENING DOORS

Up in the morning and off we go. Hi Ho, Hi Ho, it's off to work we go. George and I were buddies for more than five years. We had been working as a commercial building painters all of that time. We got along great and laughed at each others joking most hours of most days. It made the days go by a lot easier when you were sweating your fool heads off in the 100 degrees plus temperatures of summer in Phoenix Arizona.

That day we were going back to finish a job at a factory that made potato chips. The building was four stories tall and a city block long. We had been there for months repainting the whole building. When we arrived at the job site, the foreman walked us and the rest of the crew, two other guys, over to a stairwell in the back of this plant. He stopped and pointed up, saying. "See that missed spot up there." We looked up. There was a six foot by six foot spot on the wall that hadn't been painted. It was two stories up. George said, "Yea, I see it." "Well I want you to get up there and paint it," the foreman said. George asked, "How?" The scaffolding and ladders aren't here anymore, there at the other job site." The foreman responded by saying," That's for you guys to figure out."

George, the Hot Dog that he is, said, "O.K. boss, we'll get it." The foreman walks away and George headed down the hall. There in the hall was a 2-x 10, 12-ft. plank. "Here we go," George says. He then picked up one end of the plank as I grabbed the other, with the other two guys following, we start up the stairwell to the second story land-ing, directly across from the missed spot. "Grab that paint and roller," George commanded the other two guys as we were climbing the stairs. George and I laid the plank down on the landing and slid it out to the spot on the wall across the seven-foot span from the landing to the wall. It's two stories straight down from under the plank. "You guys stand on this end of the plank and I'll go out there and paint the spot," George said. Great idea George, I thought, better him than me going out there. I had courage but not like George.

There were three of us to counter balance George's 200 pounds. One guy was 275 pounds. The other was about 190 pounds, and me at 175 pounds. Didn't look like a big problem. "O.K. John," George said to the 275 pounder. "You get on the end and you guys in front of him at the rail." "O.K. George." I said. George started out onto the plank. Sitting in a position with his legs dangling over the sides of the plank and pushing the five-gallon paint pail with one gallon of paint it. So far so good. George gets to the wall and starts to roll paint on the bare spot. Well this is working out better than I expected. George with his 20 years of being a commercial building painter again showed me that he really did know what he was doing. Everything was fine, then there was a knock on the door behind John, the 275 pounder, behind me on the end of the plank.

I didn't think anything of it when all of a sudden, I started to raise in the air, the plank was lifting. What's going on?, I wondered. I glanced back and seen John stepping off the end of the plank. Someone was trying to open the door behind John. George yells and lets the paint go to grab the plank in a bear hug, face down with his arms and legs wrapping around the plank. In an instant, John realizes what we was doing and put his weight back on the plank, slamming the door on the person who was trying to open it.

The plank leveled out after it had stopped flexing like a diving board. I looked back at George, he was white as a ghost, bear hugging the plank. George yells out, "What the hell are you guys doing." The three of us looked at each other not knowing what to say to this guy that had just thought he was going to fall two stories, straight down onto a concrete floor. John replied. "Well, I was going to open this door for a guy." George said, "I'll open a door for ya." I think the door

George was talking about was the door between life and death and John knew it. As soon as George scooted back to the safety of the landing, John headed down the stairway. George took off after him. George never did catch him that day and I saw how a 275-pound man could really move when he wanted to.

The End

CHAPTER 15

▼

UP AGAINST THE WALL

"Lets get going or we're going to miss the fun." I said to Larry. We were going to a party at our friends, Ben, house in the country. It was nice day. Sun shining and I couldn't wait to get there. He had a band coming in and plenty of beer for us and about 100 people to drink. We were riding our Harley Davidson motor cycles. They were all shined up and ready to show off.

We took off. We were rolling along, out of the city and its traffic lights, into the countryside of Michigan. It certainly was nice to get to the country with clean fresh air for a change. It had been a while since either of us had a chance to do that. As we rounded a curve on this two-lane black top, half way to Ben's house, we could see the traffic starting to slow down. We could see the road signs ahead. It was a detour. The traffic was rolling at 45 mph. So we slowed to the speed of the traffic. The road started to snake and wind a bit but we did not see the necessity to slow down any further so we continued at 45 mph. The road curved to the right. We were holding the road just fine. Larry was to my immediate left. We rode side by side. A lot of riders do not ride this way because they either didn't or couldn't trust their fellow riders. The reason being, if trouble arose in the road and a quick decision had to be made you want it to be the right decision for both of you. We felt, If you couldn't trust your partners judgment when riding, you didn't ride with him.

I was in the right side of the lane. Larry was to my immediate left. We entered the curve as it went to the right. There was a concrete road divider that was coming up dividing the oncoming traffic from our side of the road at the beginning of the curve. The old concrete road dividers met the roadway flush and curved gently upward in those days. We entered the curve. Everything seemed fine that is until I noticed where I was in the lane. I was in the left side of the lane. I remember thinking, if I'm here, where is Larry? I glanced to my left. There he was, up on the dividing wall, rolling right along the side of me at a 45-degree angle. His left foot peg was just missing the concrete of the sloping divider as the centrifugal force held him to the wall at 45 mph. I thought he was going to crash right into me sending both of us into a tangled mess onto the road way. I slowed down and got back to the right side of the lane as fast as I could. Larry came rolling, smooth as silk, down off the dividing wall. I was catching my breath over what I had just witnessed. Another few miles an hour either way and he might have crashed. Larry was looking at me and laughing, just like him, the show off. All I could do was join him in his laughter. Like immortals with the wind in our face and up on two wheels tempting fate we rolled onto Ben's and had the time of our lives for we had earned it.

The End

CHAPTER 16

▼

APPLES FOR SALE

O.K., it's ready to roll. Oil in the motor, gas in the tank and air in the tires, it's been so long. I had just spent most of the winter disassembling, painting, customizing, and reassembling my 1960 Harley Davidson. Now it was ready for it's first road test, the motor was running, and sounding good. As I swung my leg over the new leather seat, my buddy Fuzzy said, "I'll follow you in the car in case it quits or something." We both laughed and I nodded. Throttle up, clutch out, I'm on my way. We were leaving the drive from his farm house in the country. The two lane black top road met me as I left the dirt drive. First gear, O.K., second gear, third and forth gear, so far so good. Up to 60 mph, cutting through the country side on a beautiful Spring day.

The road was straight as it lead to the nearest town ten miles away. I could see for a *1/4* mile ahead before the road went over the first of three small hills and dips of this two-lane black top. I did not want to push it too hard the first time out, in case it did come apart. A couple of miles up the road a car had come into view in the distance in the oncoming lane. It had its left turn signal on and was stopping to turn. No problem, I thought, there's plenty of time for it to turn before I get there, I hardly gave it a second thought. Rolling at 60 mph with the warm Spring wind in my face, I was on top of the world. It felt so good after such a long cold winter of being cooped up indoors.

It wasn't long before I noticed that the car had not made it's left turn to cross the dividing line of the road. It was just sitting there with it's left turn signal blinking. I slowed to 50mph. Closer and closer I got and still the car had not even started the turn. I had figured they must be waiting for me to pass them first. O.K. I thought. Let them feel safe and wait for me to pass then everybody will be happy. No sooner had I thought that, when I saw the car coming into my lane making it's left turn. It was less than ten car lengths in front of me. There wasn't enough room for me to either stop or clear it at this speed. I slowed to 40 mph quickly but the car was taking it's sweet old time crossing the road. I had to act fast. I was on a collision course with the car's right rear fender. I leaned to my left as hard as I could. This was going to be close, so close that it almost took my breath away but I missed it, looking down as I went by the car, like a bull fighter does when a charging bull goes by. I had seen my right foot peg just miss the shinny chrome bumper by inches. I then, just as abruptly, had to jerk the bike to the right and straighten it up to keep from going off the edge of the black top and onto the gravel shoulder where I was sure to loose my balance and crash. I was driving, but more like balancing, on the solid white line on the left side of the road now. Luckily I maintained this maneuver successfully.

I was in control and still on two wheels but on the wrong side of the road. A car, which I did not see coming, went by me on my right in the opposite direction blowing his horn, it scared the crap out of me. A second close call in the matter a second. I double checked for traffic and returned to the right side of the road, slowed down and made a right turn onto a side road. I stopped put down the kickstand then stepped off the bike. I was shaking like a leaf. My knees felt weak. Fuzzy drove up and said, "You just missed that car." "No kidding," I replied and added, "I'm going to kill that guy." I got back on the bike and started off back in the direction of where the car turned. I was black with anger and thoughts of what I was going to do to this driver. I was in a rage and felt that I would show him no mercy in my assault on him.

I approached the location of his turn, a driveway up to a farm house. I saw a sign, 'Apples For Sale'. So that was the reason the car was making the turn, to buy apples, Good God! They must have been window shopping from the road. I humored myself. I remembered thinking of the saying, 'An apple a day will keep the doctors away', and thought, yea, right. I was ready to beat this guy to a pulp until my arms got tired.

I turned up the drive with blood in my eye. There's the car, a black 1954 Ford four door. As I stopped, I saw a little old lady about 5 feet tall, white hair and with a powder blue dress, a style from the 1940's, with white lace trimming and all. She was the only customer there. The sales lady was handing her a bag of apples.

Now I knew I couldn't beat up this little old lady, so I took a deep breath and let it out to relax. Still feeling like I just had to say something. I yelled over the idling motor of my bike, "Hey lady, you know you almost killed me back there?" She turned around and looked at me as if she did not even hear the bike pull up and said, "That's O.K., you were going to fast anyway," and turned away. The saleslady was looking at me as though she was thinking, "What are you doing yelling at this poor little old lady." A growl emanated from my throat, but what could I do. The old lady was now trembling with fear. I was staring at the back of her head with a snarl on my face that I couldn't hold back. I looked away and shook my head in dismay. I was at a loss for words, put the bike in gear and slowly rolled down the driveway back to the black top road.

Her words of response resonated in my head, "I was going to fast anyway," what a defense. I could see her before the judge, "But your honor, he was going to fast, I had to do something to teach him a lesson." Well, thank God I had the riding experience to avoid her and a terrible accident. Once the wind was back in my face those thoughts melted away a few miles up the road. I was once again enjoying the sport which I loved so dearly, open road motorcycle riding.

The End

CHAPTER 17

▼

THE BLEACHERS

Here it is Saturday and nothing to do. I figured I'd go to the bar and start off with a beer. My local bar was on the corner7 I'd been going there for years. I knew most of the people that came in the place except for one that day. He came in and happened to sit down next to me on one of the few open stools at the bar.

Soon we started a light conversation. John was his name. "What kind of work do you do?" He asked. "I'm a house painter." I said. "George and I work together, do you know George?" I ask. "Oh yea, I know George all right!" He tells me. "Yea George and I go back a long time." He adds. "Oh yea." I say. "Yea, ask him about the time he drove through the bleachers with his Corvette at the High School." He replies. I had known George to be a Hot Dog and he did tell me he had a Corvette once but he never told me about driving through any bleachers. I could just picture the wreckage of a mangled Vet wrapped around some high school bleachers. I couldn't wait to see him and rib him about it.

I eventually went home and found George there. I walked in the door and said. "I saw an old friend of yours at the bar today." "Oh yea, who?" he asks. "A guy named John, he told me to ask you about the time you drove through some bleachers at a High School." I reply. George looks at me calmly and asks. "Which time?" "Which time, what do you mean, which time?" I start to laugh as I asked him. "Yea, I did it three times." He states. "Three times, you drove cars into bleachers?" This was too much to believe, even coming from George. I wasn't sure about what I was about to hear.

"No, I said I drove through them. I'd get some speed up for the thrill of it and drive through them, through the metal beams that held them up. I didn't drive and crash into them.". He says and adds. "Yes and I did it three times while in High School." Oh my God, he drove through the bleachers not into them. Now he was laughing. "You have to listen what people say, not what you think they say." He states. "Man, I thought." He stops me and says. "Yea I know what you thought. Then we both were laughing.

The End

The End

0-595-25743-7